IMAGES
of Scotland

RANGERS
FOOTBALL CLUB
1872-1964

IMAGES
of Scotland

RANGERS
FOOTBALL CLUB
1872-1964

Compiled by
Robert McElroy

TEMPUS

First published 1998
Copyright © Robert McElroy, 1998

Tempus Publishing Limited
The Mill, Brimscombe Port,
Stroud, Gloucestershire, GL5 2QG

ISBN 0 7524 1191 8

Typesetting and origination by
Tempus Publishing Limited
Printed in Great Britain by
Midway Clark Printing, Wiltshire

Contents

Rangers 4 Raith Rovers 3 (17 August 1957). Alex Scott is foiled by the combined efforts of Young, Drummond and Pollard of Raith Rovers.

Introduction

This is a unique collection of photographs of a unique football club. The story of The Rangers Football Club is one of sport's most romantic tales – from humble origins amongst the public pitches of the Fleshers' Haugh on Glasgow Green in 1872, to the multi-million pound organisation of today.

The club was founded by four young Glasgow students – the brothers Moses and Peter McNeil, Peter Campbell and William McBeath – all of whom hailed from villages along the Gare Loch from Rhu to Garelochhead, some thirty miles from Glasgow.

Those four students had no pitch, no ball, no strips (they played their inaugural game in their ordinary clothes) and yet they survived. After a long, grim struggle, Rangers Football Club eventually prospered (owing their popularity at least in part to their very youthfulness), growing as the City of Glasgow did with the Industrial Revolution of the nineteenth century and the introduction of heavy industry to the Clyde. As football developed from a sporting pastime to the popular game of the masses, the clubs of the major cities took over from the amateur sides, whose Corinthian spirit had done so much to establish the sport. In Scotland, Glasgow in the form of Rangers and Celtic rested power from the hands of Queen's Park and the village teams of Dunbartonshire – Renton, Vale Of Leven, and Dumbarton themselves.

As the twentieth century unfolded, Rangers clearly established themselves as the most successful club in the land, carving out a place at the very heart of the nation. The club became as much a part of the Scottish culture and heritage as the Church of Scotland, the Royal and Ancient Golf Club of St Andrews, and the unique Scottish Legal system. This collection of photographs traces the story of the club from those early days on Glasgow Green to their first ground at Burnbank, to Kinning Park and on to the Ibrox area, the site of the First Ibrox, which is adjacent to the present magnificent stadium that has been their home since December 1899.

Many Rangers legends are pictured here, many memorable games are recalled, the triumphs and tragedies that have encompassed the story of the Rangers. The great striving to annexe the 'Blue Riband' of the nineteenth century, the Scottish Cup, finally secured in 1894 with a 3-1 triumph over Celtic after two losing finals in 1877 and 1879. The long barren twenty-five years when all were swept before the 'Light Blues' save for that same national trophy, finally ending when Rangers crushed their great rivals Celtic aside 4 - 0 in 1928 in a game that will live forever in Ibrox folklore. The Ibrox side of the early 1960s, still regarded by many friends of Rangers as the greatest of them all, culminating in the Triple Crown Triumph of 1963/4 and the memorable 3 - 1 Scottish Cup Final win over Dundee, a game which to this day is rated as the finest final ever witnessed.

No book of this nature can of course record every aspect of the Rangers Archives. The dearth of photographs from the early years makes such a task well - nigh impossible, but we do offer a window of opportunity to view selected scenes from the history of one of sport's giants, a montage of action shots and profiles that reflect a proud and distinguished past.

Every book of course must have an ending, a final chapter, and in drawing our line at the triumphant team of the early 1960s, and at the 1964 Scottish Cup Final, we fully appreciate that this may disappoint many readers who will recall with great fondness the two Treble triumphs of Jock Wallace and of course the Souness Revolution of 1986, not to mention the glory of the club's second 'Nine In A Row' under Walter Smith, but perhaps that can await another volume...

One
The Early Days

The imposing marble-floored and wood-panelled entrance to Ibrox Stadium.

In West End Park, Glasgow

Glasgow's West End Park, where four young students hailing from the Gare Loch decided to form a football club in 1872. The four founders were Moses and Peter McNeil, Peter Campbell and William McBeath. To Moses goes the credit for the naming of the club *Rangers*.

After three years playing on the public pitches of Flesher's Haugh at Glasgow Green, Rangers moved to a home of their own at Burnbank, off Great Western Road, for just one season. Pictured here is the site of their ground for Season 1875/76.

Rangers' Scottish Cup Final line-up for the 1877 tie with the Vale Of Leven at Hamilton Crescent, Glasgow. After two 1-1 draws, Rangers lost the second replay 3-2 at the First Hampden Park. Included in the team are two of the original founders, Moses McNeil and Peter Campbell. This series of three games brought the young Glasgow club into greater prominence, challenging their 'mighty' opponents from the 'Cradle of Football' – Dunbartonshire. The nickname of 'Light Blues' originates from this time – Vale of Leven wore dark blue shirts, and the final was billed as the 'Light Blues' versus the 'Dark Blues'.

The West of Scotland ground at Hamilton Crescent, site of Rangers' first Scottish Cup Final, and also of the first Scotland *v*. England international in 1872.

Tom Vallance (1872-1884). President 1883-1889. A founding member, and club captain for nine seasons, Tom Vallance was a powerful left-back, a noted athlete and a gifted artist.

Rangers farewell gathering at Kinning Park on 26 February 1887. The ground had been their home since 1876 and was closed with a game between the 'Ancients' and the 'Moderns'.

From 1887-1899, Rangers played at the first Ibrox Park, adjacent to the present stadium, with its' eastern boundary on Copland Road. Pictured here in front of the pavilion are the players and officials on 8 September 1888, when Rangers drew 1-1 with a touring Canadian side.

The first Rangers team to win the Scottish Cup in 1894. Rangers campaign that season consisted of : R1 Cowlairs (H) 8-0; R2 Leith Athletic (H) 2-0; QF Clyde (A) 5-0; SF Queen's Park (H) 1-1; (A) 3-1; Final Celtic (Second Hampden Park) 3-1 . Rangers' scorers were Hugh McCreadie, J.B. Barker and John MacPherson. Also pictured is the Glasgow Cup. The players are, from left to right, back row: H. McCreadie, J. Steel, J. Taylor (Trainer), N. Smith, D. Haddow, D. Mitchell. Sitting: A. McCreadie, D. Boyd, W. Wilton (Secretary), J. Drummond, J. MacPherson, J. Barker. Front row: R. Marshall, J. Gray.

Rangers postcard from the early 1900s.

A Rangers team-group from 1895/96 – but this is of the Ibrox XI who played in Junior football. From left to right, back row: A. Robb, P. McLaren, J.M. McLean (Secretary), A. Barr, S. Bryson. Middle row: P. Rennie, A. Binnie, G. Lyon, J. Yullie, D. Chisholm, J. Greig, D.M. McLeod. Front row: D. Barclay, J. McNeish, J. McDonald, W. Prentice.

John Robertson Gow (1885-1891). President 1896-98. A versatile, elusive forward of athletic and graceful ability, J.R. Gow served the club in various capacities. He was also a famed Scottish athlete as a sprinter and hurdler, and his brother Donald Robertson was a Ranger too.

The 'Three-Cup team' of 1896/97. Rangers won the Glasgow Cup 2-1 against Celtic following a 1-1 draw; the Scottish Cup 5-1 against Dumbarton; and the Glasgow Merchants' Charity Cup against the Third Lanark Rifle Volunteers, 6-1. Both the Scottish and charity finals were played at the Second Hampden Park (later the Second Cathkin Park), and the Glasgow Cup Final at First Cathkin.

A record that in all probability will never be equalled anywhere in world football – the 1898/99 squad that won every League game – a 100 per cent record.

William Wilton – Honorary Match Secretary 1889/1899; Manager 1899-1920. The club's first manager, and a distinguished administrator whose untimely death was a great loss to Rangers.

An illustration of how the Press viewed the Rangers *v*. Celtic game of 1898.

James Henderson – President 1898/99; Chairman 1899-1912. The club's first chairman following the adoption of limited liability.

John McPherson (1890-1902). Director 1907-26. At Rangers' 50th Anniversary Dinner, 'Kitey' was described as the finest of all the players to have played for the club in its' first fifty years. A versatile performer who played in almost every position for the club, including goal, but primarily an inside forward with an astute tactical brain.

The 1902 Ibrox Disaster. Twenty-five spectators plunged to their deaths when the wooden terracing collapsed during the Scotland v. England international. The disaster would have far-reaching consequences regarding stadium construction. Rangers had moved to their new ground just three years earlier.

Jock Drummond (1892-1904). A full-back, strong on either flank, Jock Drummond was perhaps the last outfield player in first class football to wear a cap. Capped fourteen times for Scotland, and went on to become a director of Falkirk.

Nicol Smith (1893-1905). Nicol Smith's full-back partnership with Jock Drummond was one of the greatest in Rangers' history. Smith died tragically young at the age of just thirty-one from enteric fever, whilst still a Rangers player.

Neil Gibson (1894-1904). A cultured, skillful wing half regarded by historians as one of the all-time greats of Scottish Football, perhaps greater even than Jim Baxter, who played in the same position. Three sons became professional footballers, including one (James) who was a 'Wembley Wizard' in 1928.

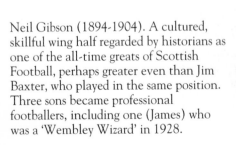

Robert Cumming Hamilton (1897-1906; 1907-08). A prolific goalscorer, Hamilton's tally of thirty-six in Old Firm games is a record which stands to this day.

Jackie Robertson (1899-1905). Powerful wing half, and a forceful, driving player with a thunderous shot.

The Rangers Brake Club-the equivalent of today's supporters' clubs. The player portrayed in the banner is that of Ibrox legend Jimmy Gordon.

A badge of the old Rangers Brake Club Association.

Two

The Creation of Legends

R.S. McColl (1904-1907). In later years a most successful businessman in the confectionary trade. Centre forward, amongst the most famous footballers of the era leading up to the First World War. A prolific goalscorer and a skilful player, he was the first professional to return to Queen's Park.

Ibrox in the early years of the twentieth century.

Tom Sinclair (1904-1907). A goalkeeper, whose record in the 1906/07 season would take some beating, winning a Scottish 2nd XI Cup winners' medal with Rangers, a Glasgow Cup winners' medal with Celtic, and a League Championship medal with Newcastle United.

Rangers Team Group 1908/09. From left to right, back row: Robert Noble, James Jackson, Alex Bennett, James E. Gordon. Middle row: Henry G. Rennie, James Galt, David Taylor, John Macdonald, John McArthur, George Law, Thomas Murray. Front row: Alex Craig, William Macpherson, Thomas Gilchrist, R.G. Campbell, James Sharp, George T. Livingstone, Alex Smith.

Willie Reid (1909-20). A prolific goalscorer in the period before and during the First World War, Willie Reid is pictured here in the uniform of the Royal Field Artillery 52nd (Lowland) Division. In Rangers' long and proud history, only three men have scored more League goals than Reid – Jimmy Smith, Ally McCoist and Bob McPhail. He died in May 1964, ten days after his eightieth birthday.

Willie Reid threatens the Clyde goal at Shawfield on 10 February 1912, before a staggering record attendance for that ground of 52,000. Clyde were leading 3-1 when spectator encroachment (presumably due to the massive overcrowding) forced the abandonment of the game. Rangers conceded the tie.

Douglas Park, Hamilton is the venue on 8 February 1913, as Brown, Logan and Galt prepare for a Rangers free kick. Garrett, Garvie and Rippon are the Accies in view. The result was a 1-1 draw, with Willie Reid the scorer. Rangers won the replay 2-0.

Rangers Team Group 1911/12. From left to right, back row: J. Wilson (Trainer), G. Ormond, G. Chapman, R.G. Campbell, J. Galt, W. Hogg, J. Cameron, W. Reid, A. Richmond, A. Gibson, G. Law. Middle row: A. Bodin, J. Gordon, G. Wadell, J. Bowie, H. Lock, A. Bennett, R. Parker, A. Smith. Front row: R. Brown, J. Paterson, J. Goodwin, A. Brown, J. Hendry.

Royalty at Ibrox. His Majesty King George V held an Investiture at Ibrox on 18 September 1917.

Dr James Paterson (1911-20). A winger of great consistency, his medical practice took him to London, where he played with great distinction for Arsenal. A worthy link in the chain which passed from Alec Smith to Alan Morton.

Alec Smith (1894-1915). A record of longevity surpassed only by Dougie Gray, Smith's twenty-one years as a Ranger encompassed the first great era enjoyed by the club. He was granted no fewer than four benefit matches.

A League Championship medal won by Alec Smith, one of seven. The legendary winger also won three Scottish Cup winners' medals, and the Exhibition Cup of 1901. Alec was an ever-present in the 1898/99 team that won every game.

Willie Kivlichan (1905-1907). Played for both Rangers and Celtic. A medical practioner in later years.

Alex Craig (1905-1911). Irish International full-back, who played in both games of the inconclusive 1909 Scottish Cup Final, and was involved in the famous 1905 Scottish Cup tie at Celtic Park, abandoned following Craig's clash with Jimmy Quinn. Celtic subsequently conceded the tie. It would be ninety-three years before Rangers again defeated Celtic at Celtic Park in a Scottish Cup tie.

James Stark (1902-1907; 1908 - 1910). Centre half and captain, the driving-force behind the team that won the Glasgow International Exhibition Cup in 1901, defeating Celtic 3-1 at Gilmorehill. His duels with Jimmy Quinn of Celtic became a part of Old Firm folklore.

James Galt (1906-1914). A
methodical, hard-working wing
half who also played for Everton,
his career coming to an end
during the First World War when
he suffered severe shell-shock.
Owned a tobacconist/stationery
shop in Govan and had other
business interests in billiards and
motor cars.

Alex Bennett (1908-1916).
Inside forward, unquestionably
the finest player to have played
for both Rangers and Celtic. His
heart was always at Ibrox.

Billy Hogg (1909-1913). A powerful winger, and an English internationalist (the first to play for Rangers). Signed for £100 from Sunderland, Billy had a 'devil-may-care' attitude, giving the impression of a 'great big boy, bubbling over with animal spirit'.

Herbert Lock (1909-20). Outstanding English goalkeeper, signed from Southampton. A prolonged period as Rangers' custodian, only the consistency of Sam Hardy denied Lock international recognition. A daring, sometimes reckless goalkeeper.

James Bowie (1910-22). Chairman 1934-47. Scottish League President 1939-46. A creative wing half or inside forward.

Tommy Cairns (1913-27). A resolute, hard-working inside forward and club captain for a prolonged period. Won every honour bar a Scottish Cup winners' medal with Rangers, his haul even included a Scottish Junior Cup winners' medal with Burnbank Athletic in 1911.

James Blair (1916-19). Full-back. Won a League Championship medal in 1917/18, Glasgow Cup winners' medals in 1917 and 1918, and a Charity Cup medal in 1919 – Wiliam Wilton's last trophy success for Rangers.

Bert Manderson (1915-27). Belfast-born full-back of considerable pace, his partnership with Willie McCandless was an enduring one.

Andy Cunningham (1915-29). One of the outstanding players of the 1920s, an inside forward of power, a goalscorer supreme and also a master of the sweeping through-pass. The oldest debutant in the Football League when he signed for Newcastle United in 1929 – but at least he had stayed a Ranger long enough to win a Scottish Cup badge.

Tommy Muirhead (1917-30). A versatile player at wing half or inside forward, injury deprived club captain Muirhead of the chance to lead his team in the 1928 Scottish Cup Final, with Meiklejohn deputising. The rest is history.

James 'Fister' Walls (1918-24). A wing half whose career was badly compromised by an injury received at Shawfield.

William J. 'Daddler' Aitken (1918-19). A winger who scored in a Glasgow Cup Final win over Celtic (2-0) and went on to achieve legendary status with Newcastle United.

An unusual crowd scene at a Rangers-an Alloa Athletic Scottish Cup tie in 1921. A crowd of 60,000 watched a goalless draw.

The Ibrox Pavilion as it used to be, *c.* 1920.

Rangers win the Scottish Cup replay against Alloa 4-1.

Rangers v Dumbarton in 1920, with Andy Cunningham and Tommy Cairns posing a threat to the Sons' defence. The Light Blues won 1-0.

After eliminating Celtic in the Quarter-finals, Rangers were regarded as certainties to win the national trophy for the first time in seventeen years, only to lose to Albion Rovers after three Semi-final matches. The Ibrox tie with Celtic featured on this page sees Tommy Muirhead and James Paterson challenge the Celtic goal.

Tommy Muirhead is about to score the game's only goal. A record attendance of 85,000 was present.

Rangers Team Group 1920/21. From left to right, back row: J. Smith, G. Queen, D. Meiklejohn, H. Lawson, Sutherland (from Broxburn), T. McDonald, R. McMillan. Middle row: G. Livingstone (Trainer), J. Walls, T. Reid, H. Lock, R. Manderson, W. Robb, H. McKenna, A. Archibald. Front row: E. Laird, A. Dixon, G. Henderson, J. Bowie, J. Low, T.Muirhead, A. Johnstone, A. Morton.

Willie McCandless (1920-30). An Ulsterman, McCandless was a popular full-back who was given the nickname of 'Bucksy'.

Carl Hansen (1921-24). Danish internationalist nicknamed 'Little Shoemaker' (his profession), who impressed when he played against the touring Ibrox men. Made an immediate impact on his debut, netting three in a 3-2 win over Queen's Park in the Lord Provosts' Rent Relief Fund Tournament. A broken leg hindered his prospects at Ibrox, but he was always a popular visitor in later years. Imprisoned by occupying German forces in Copenhagen during The Second World War.

J.R. Smith (1922). Centre forward who played just a handful of games, but wrote himself into the record books with sixty-six league goals for Ayr United in 1927/28.

Rangers Team Group 1922/23. From left to right, back row: M. McDonald, T. Reid, A. Kirkwood, J. Walls, J. Kilpatrick, R. Ireland, J. Rollo, F. Roberts, W. McCandless. Middle row: W. Struth (Manager), T. Hamilton, D. Meiklejohn, I. Jamieson, T. Craig, J. Nicholson, G. Henderson, A. Johnston, A. Dixon, H. Lawson, W. Robb, G.T. Livingstone (Trainer). Front row: A. Archibald, T. Muirhead, T. Cairns, R. Manderson (Captain), A. Cunningham, A.L. Morton, C. Hansen.

Geordie Henderson – still regarded to this day by some old-timers as the finest centre to play for Rangers – heads a Sandy Archibald corner home in a Scottish Cup tie at Shawfield in 1923. Rangers won 4-0.

Blue Heaven – Rangers overwhelm Celtic 4-1 in the Glasgow Cup Final of 4 October 1924 at Celtic Park. Captain Tommy Cairns instructs his players to ease off after the fourth goal! Here, John Jamieson, Tully Craig, Willie Robb, Arthur Dixon and Bert Manderson foil a Celtic attack.

Five months later, and Celtic defeat Rangers 5-0 in the Scottish Cup Sem-final! Tommy Cairns' thoughts remain unpublished....

Sandy Archibald (on the left) scores against Hamilton Accies in 1927. Rangers won 4-0.

Jimmy Fleming (in white) threatens the Cowdenbeath goal in 1928, as Rangers win 4-2.

It's the 1928 Scottish Cup Final, and the most famous penalty in Old Firm history, as Willie McStay punches the ball off (or behind) the line. Rangers captain David Meiklejohn scores, the Light-Blues win 4-0, and the Scottish Cup is Ibrox-bound for the first time in twenty-five years.

At last – David Meiklejohn holds the Scottish Cup aloft.

Shawfield 1929, and Sandy Archibald helps Tommy Muirhead to his feet after scoring the opening goal in a 2-0 win.

George Brown and James Marshall rush the Cowdenbeath goal in a 1930 Scottish Cup tie, which ended in a shock 2-2 draw. Rangers won the Central Park replay 3-0, and went on to lift the trophy for the second time in three years.

A record attendance at Tynecastle of 53,496 in 1932 saw Jimmy Fleming's header set up James Marshall for the only goal.

Rangers are on the way to Scottish Cup success again, this time for the third time in five years, and here is the legendary Bob McPhail in an unconventional pose at Celtic Park, as Rangers win 5-2 against Hamilton.

Dr James Marshall (1925-34). A match-winner with many memorable goals, 'Doc' Marshall followed the path of James Paterson in moving to London with his medical practice – this time to West Ham.

Jimmy Fleming (1925-34). A prolific goalscorer, holding the Scottish Cup record for the club, with forty-four goals.

Dougie Gray (1925-47). The longest-serving Ranger of them all. A full-back who holds the appearance record for the club. Born Alford, Aberdeenshire, Gray's 940 games for the club encompassed sixteen League Championship and six Scottish Cup winners' medals.

British Cup Winners Challenge, 14 September 1932 - Rangers 4 Newcastle United 1.

Rangers Team Group 1933/34. From left to right, back row: J. Dawson, T. Gillick, T. Craig, T. Hamilton, R. McDonald, J. Fleming, G. Jenkins. Middle row: W. Struth (Manager), J. Marshall, A. Cheyne, J. Simpson, J. Kennedy, J. Smith, J. Drysdale, R. McPhail, A. Dixon (Trainer). Front row: R. Main, A. McCauley, D. Gray, A. Venters, D. Meiklejohn (Captain), T. Hart, G. Brown, A. Archibald, W. G. Nicholson.

Andy Archibald (1917-34). Right-winger who holds the record for the greatest number of League appearances by a Rangers player, if one excludes Dougie Gray's wartime games. Substantially built, he scored two spectacular goals in the 1928 Scottish Cup Final.

Bob McPhail (1927-40). With 230 League goals, the club's record league goalscorer until the coming of Ally McCoist, excluding the wartime goals of Jimmy Smith. A strong, bustling inside forward who won seven Scottish Cup winners' medals, including one with Airdrieonians.

Jimmy Smith (1928-46). A strong, bustling centre forward, whose record of 299 League goals (including wartime) is unlikely to ever be broken. In later years, trainer and chief scout at Ibrox.

Jimmy Simpson (1927-40). Centre half, a mainstay of the great team of the 1930's. Father of Celtic goalkeeper Ronnie Simpson.

George Brown (1929-42). A polished wing half, a teacher by profession, and a director of the club in later years. Brown is seen here shaking hands with the future king.

Alex Venters (1933-46). Chunky inside forward who was first capped whilst at Cowdenbeath. Scored a phenomenal amount of goals for Rangers, and was a prolific marksman against Celtic. Worked as a compositor in the printing industry, and died at tragically young age of forty-five.

David Kinnear (1934-46). War interrupted the career of this winger. Rangers' trainer from 1956-70.

Rangers Football Club, 1934.

Ibrox, 1934 and Jimmy Smith beats his namesake Steve for the only goal, as Rangers win the Scottish Cup for the fourth time in seven years.

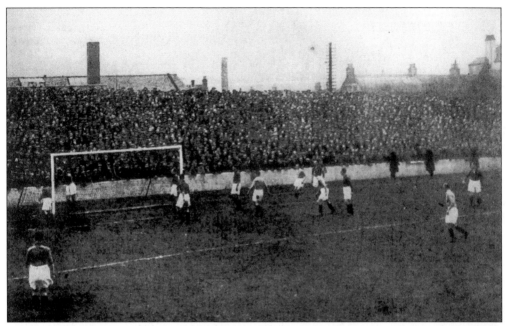

Rangers blitzed Motherwell 4-1 at Fir Park in 1935 on their way to retaining the silverware for the first time in the twentieth century, and here Alan McClory cuts out a Torry Gillick cross.

Rangers again won 1-0 against Aberdeen, this time at Pittodrie in 1936.

Jimmy Smith and Bob McPhail challenge in a 3-0 Semi-final win over Clyde, as Rangers go for a third Scottish Cup success in 1936. Goalscorers were David Meiklejohn, Bob McPhail and Bobby Main, before an attendance of 56,243. A first-minute McPhail goal ensured the Light Blues a treble of Scottish Cup triumphs, with a 1-0 victory over Third Lanark.

Scotland 2 Germany 0 in 1936, and the Nazi Swastika flies over Ibrox.

For King and Empire – the opening ceremony of the 1938 Empire Ehibition. King George VI and Queen Elizabeth arrive at Ibrox Stadium to officially declare the exhibition (watched by 100,000 spectators) open.

Rangers hopes of a 'Royal Blue' triumph disintegrate, as they fall at the first hurdle 2-0 to Everton, and here Jimmy Simpson (in hoops) clears from Tommy Lawton. Everton would eventually lose 1-0 to Celtic in the final.

A record attendance of 118,730 that will surely stand for all time, watch, as Rangers defeat Celtic 2-1 on 2 January 1939, and here Alex Venters nets the winning goal, beating Joe Kennaway.

'The Wee Society Man' aka 'The Wee Blue Devil' – perhaps the most famous Rangers player of them all – Alan Lauder Morton. His portrait hangs in oils in the imposing oak - panelled marble entrance to Ibrox Stadium. Morton wore the Light Blue with distinction from 1920-33, and was a director of the club from 1933 until his death in 1971.

Jerry Dawson – The Prince of Goalkeepers (1929-45). There are many who to this day will rate Jerry Dawson as the greatest of all goalkeepers. Here he is introduced to HRH The Duke of Gloucester, prior to the 1939 Scotland v. England international. England won 2-1.

Dawson lies beaten here – caught unawares in the first minute of the famous Rangers - Dinamo Moscow game in 1945, which finished 2-2.

Three Rangers legends – Jimmy Smith, Jerry Dawson and Bob McPhail.

Rangers 2 Dinamo Moscow 2 (November 1945).

An aerial view of Ibrox Stadium, *c*. 1950.

Three
The Fifties

'A Winter's Tale' as Rangers destroy Cowdenbeath 8-0 in a Scottish Cup tie on 11 February 1950. Billy Williamson is seen here scoring. Earlier that same season, the Fifers made history by becoming the first Division Two team to win at Ibrox, 3-2 in a League Cup fixture.

A Scottish Cup Quarter-final with Raith Rovers took three games to decide before Rangers won 2-0. Rangers' strip in this picture is red with a white and blue band.

Bobby Brown and George Young combine to foil an East Fife attack in a 2-2 draw on 8 April 1950.

A post-war League record attendance of 101,200 saw Rangers and Hibernian draw 0-0 in a crucial fixture on 29 April 1950. The draw enabled Rangers to clinch the Championship two days later at Cathkin Park, with a 2-2 draw.

The crowd packs Ibrox.

Jimmy Cowan foils Willie Thornton as Rangers defeat Morton 2-0 on 9 December 1950.

A Billy Simpson hat-trick helped Rangers defeat East Fife 5-0 on 23 December 1950.

Rangers Team Group 1951/52. From left to right, back row: I. McColl. W. Boyd, J. Little, A. Elliot, R. Brown, G. Niven, J. Johnson, W. Rae, J. Forbes, E. Rutherford, A. Miller. Middle row: J. Smith (Trainer), L. Blyth, W. Woodburn, A. McPhail, W. Waddell, W. McCulloch, W. Paton, W. Findlay, D. Stanners, R. Dunlop, J. Prentice, J. Pryde, W. Thorton, J. Craven (Assistant Trainer). Front row: W. Struth (Director, Manager), W. Beckett, J. Hubbard, W. Simpson, S. Cox, R. Simpson, G. Young, D. Marshall, J. Woods, G. Scobbie, J. Shaw, A. Simpson, W. Williamson.

Rangers 4 East Fife 1 (25 August 1951).

Dunfermline goalkeeper Moodie defies Thornton as Rangers defeat the 'Pars' 3-1 in a League Cup Quarter-final tie on 19 September 1951.

Rangers and Celtic never meet in Semi-finals, or so the cynics say. Well, they did in 1951, and here Willie Thornton challenges Sean Fallon and Bobby Evans, as Rangers triumph 3-0 to surge through to the League Cup Final.

It was Dundee's day in the 1951 League Cup Final, however, winning 3-2 for their first major trophy success since 1910, and in this picture Bill Brown defies the combined efforts of Willie Thornton and Joe Johnson.

Rangers 2 Hearts 0 (20 October 1951).

A one-off tournament held in Glasgow to celebrate the coronation of Her Majesty Queen Elizabeth II in 1953, saw Rangers succumb 2-1 to Manchester United at Hampden, with Stan Pearson seen here scoring for the Old Trafford side. Niven, Little and Woodburn are onlookers. Celtic eventually won the Coronation Cup, defeating Hibernian 2-0 in the final.

The famous castellated Press Box (sadly no longer with us) is prominent here as George Niven and Johnny Little clear up an East Fife attack at Ibrox on 17 October 1953. Rangers won 2-0.

Rangers 3 Partick Thistle 0 (5 September 1953).

Bobby Howitt nets the second goal for Partick Thistle in a shock 2-0 win over Rangers on 10 October, 1953 in the League Cup Semi-final.

How one cartoonist viewed Thistle's win.

Rangers 0 Hearts 1 (31 October 1953). George Niven secures a cross ball as Young and Little guard the line with Hearts' goalscorer supreme Jimmy Wardhaugh waiting to pounce. Note the floodlighting system on the roof of the covered terracing.

Partick Thistle 0 Rangers 1 (19 December 1953).

George Young clears up a Dundee attack in this 2-0 win on 6 February 1954 at Ibrox.

Rangers 4 Berwick Rangers 0 (Scottish Cup, 13 March 1954).

Rangers and Kilmarnock fight out a 2-2 Scottish Cup draw at Ibrox on 13 February 1954. Note the new floodlighting system, including the pylon in the west terracing corner.

Four days later, Rangers win 3-1 at Rugby Park, and here Willie Paton outjumps Bob Thyne to score in front of a record attendance of 33,545.

Disaster at Hampden – the 1954 Scottish Cup Semi-final – Aberdeen 6 Rangers 0. Fred Martin secures the ball despite the attention of Billy Simpson and Johnny Hubbard.

Rangers 3 Falkirk 0 (20 April 1954). Billy Simpson stoops to head home.

Rangers in Montreal, 1954. Rangers played nine games during their 1954 tour of North America.

May 16 *v*. Chelsea (played Montreal, Quebec)   1-0
     19 *v*. Hamilton and District All-Stars   6-0
     22 *v*. Ontario All-Stars   4-1
     24 *v*. British Columbia Mainland All-Stars   9-0
     26 *v*. Victoria   7-0
     29 *v*. Vancouver All-Stars   3-0
June 2 *v*. Manitoba All-Stars   5-0
      5 *v*. Chelsea (played Toronto, Ontario)   1-4
      6 *v*. Chelsea (played New York)   0-0

The Rangers Sports. Always a popular athletics meeting, The Rangers Sports were held at Ibrox until 1962, and the scenes depicted here are from the 1954 event.

Bill Struth – Rangers' Trainer
1914-20; Manager 1920-1954.

James Scotland Symon –
Rangers' Player 1938-47;
Manager 1954-1967.

A rare picture of the two managers pictured together at the Rangers Sports in 1954. Note the extension being constructed on the covered terracing in the background.

Newly appointed Rangers' boss Scot Symon is pictured here with directors George Brown and Alan Morton.

Willie Thorton (1937-54). 'One who wore the light blue to the honour of himself and the club he served'. An outstanding sportsman and a fine centre forward who was deadly in the air. Awarded the Military Medal in the Second World War, his name lives on in the Thornton Suite at the stadium. The first player in the post-war era to score 100 League goals. Manager of Dundee and Partick Thistle, and assistant manager of Rangers.

Willie Woodburn (1937-55). There are many who to this day would rate Willie Woodburn as the finest centre half to play for Rangers. A stylish and dominant pivot, he had a stormy career which culminated in a *sine die* suspension in 1954, a ban which today appears harsh in the extreme, and that in law would be totally unsustainable. Woodburn had been ordered off just four times in his career.

Jimmy Duncanson (1938-50). A devastating forward for Rangers, he scored the club's 4,000th League goal against Dundee on Christmas Day 1947. Only R.C. Hamilton and Ally McCoist scored more goals against Celtic than Duncanson.

Jock Shaw (1938-54). 'Tiger Shaw' was a durable, hard tackling full-back, who played on past his fortieth birthday. Club captain of the 'Iron Curtain' team, he captained Scotland on all four of his post-war international appearances.

Willie Waddell (1938-56). One of the great Ibrox careers. As player, manager, general manager and managing director, Willie Waddell served the club for half a century. A powerful winger of no little skill, his partnership with Thornton was the springboard from defence for the 'Iron Curtain' team. As manager, he led Rangers to European success in 1972, and coped with the aftermath of the 1971 Ibrox Disaster. As an administrator, his vision created the new Ibrox Stadium of today. His name lives on in the Waddell Suite at Ibrox.

Ian McColl (1945-61). A skillful wing half. A graduate of Glasgow University, and an engineer by profession, Ian McColl won six League Championship and five Scottish Cup medals at Ibrox. Successor to George Young as club captain, and manager of Scotland 1961-65 – a period of outstanding success for the national side.

Sammy Cox (1946-56). Tough tackling left-back or left half, Sammy Cox was an integral part of the 'Iron Curtain'. His duels with Charlie Tully of Celtic were the very stuff of legend.

Johnny Hubbard (1949-58). A South African born and bred, the little winger was the ultimate penalty expert, converting fifty-four out of fifty-seven for Rangers.

Billy Simpson (1950-59). Signed from Linfield in 1950, Ulsterman Billy Simpson played in all three inside forward positions for Rangers. The scorer of 163 goals in 239 games, including a century of League goals

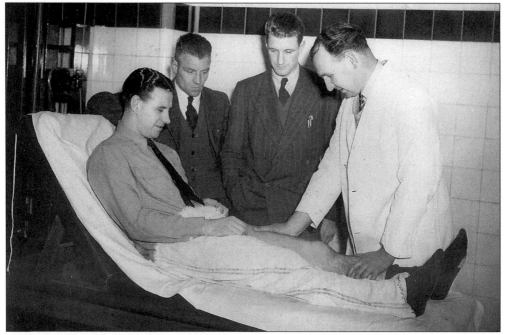

The Treatment Room at Ibrox, housing four Rangers legends in this photograph. From left to right: Willie Waddell, Jock Shaw, Willie Woodburn and Jimmy Smith.

A mid-fifties clash with Motherwell, bringing George Niven and George Young to the fore.

Willie Paton scores for the Light Blues in this League Cup tie on 25 September 1954, but it's not enough to prevent Motherwell going through.

Glasgow Cup Final, 1954/55. Partick Thistle 2 Rangers 0.

Fred Martin foils Billy Simpson and Derek Grierson, but Rangers beat Aberdeen 3-1 on 11 December 1954.

Floodlight football brought the opportunity to invite the continentals, and Rangers defeated Rapid Vienna 1-0 on 15 December 1954.

Rangers 2 East Fife 0 (8 January 1955).

For the second successive year, Rangers' Scottish Cup dreams perished at the hands of Aberdeen – this time in treacherous conditions at Pittodrie (1-2) on 19 February 1955.

George Niven repels a Celtic raid in a Charity Cup tie at Celtic Park on 7 May 1955. Rangers won 1-0 thanks to Billy Simpson.

Bobby Brown (1946-56). Signed on the same day as Sammy Cox, Brown was a spectacular athletic goalkeeper who has the singular honour of being the last amateur to represent Scotland at full international level. He also represented the Royal Navy during the Second World War when serving with the Fleet Air Arm. In later years, manager of both St Johnstone and Scotland.

George Young (1941-57). A colossus of a player. Right-back or centre half, he succeeded Jock Shaw as club captain, and indeed captained Scotland a record forty-eight times. A true leader of men and an absolute gentleman. One of the all-time greats in Rangers' history.

Third Time Lucky! Rangers defeat Aberdeen in a 1956 Scottish Cup-tie, 2-1. Alex Scott opens the scoring despite the presence of three 'Dons' defenders.

Rangers 3 Ayr United 1 (29 September 1956). Derek Grierson and Max Murray (on the ground) are foiled on this occasion.

Don Kichenbrand (1955-57). South African, nicknamed 'The Rhino'. A strong, bustling centre forward who split the Rangers fans down the middle. A record of thirty goals in thirty-seven games was a fair innings.

Sammy Baird (1955-60). Wing half or inside forward, Sammy Baird revelled in European ties and in Old Firm encounters.

Max Murray (1955-62). Another controversial centre forward who divided the fans, Murray nevertheless was leading League scorer for three consecutive seasons in the fifties. He scored 121 goals in 154 appearances.

Alex Scott (1955-63). A flying winger of great pace and no little skill, Alex Scott made a dream debut on 9 March 1955, scoring a hat-trick in a 4-1 win over Falkirk. Scoring twelve goals in European competition, Scott won League and Cup medals on both sides of the border, in England with Everton.

Harold Davis (1956-64). A veteran of the Korean War, Harry Davis was the 'Iron Man' of the Rangers side. A hard-tackling wing half, and in later years a coach at Ibrox.

willie telfer

Centre-half

RANGERS
& SCOTLAND

Willie Telfer (1957-60). A surprise signing following the catastrophic League Cup Final defeat of 1957, Telfer was an experienced centre half viewed as a stopgap, who let no-one down.

Celtic 4 Rangers 4, 1957 Scottish Cup tie. Rangers come back from the dead at Parkhead with two goals in the last six minutes. Max Murray turns away to the acclaim of his teammates Billy Simpson and Sammy Baird, having scored the fourth, and equalising goal.

The Ibrox replay, which Celtic won 2-0. Here, George Niven shepherds a crossball safely wide of goal.

A seven-goal thriller, as Rangers just get the better of Raith Rovers in a League Cup-tie on 17 August 1957. Here, Murray and Baird are just denied by Drummond.

Rangers 4 Queen Of The South 2 (7 September 1957). Kichenbrand is foiled by Henderson.

Billy Simpson deflects a Hubbard corner past Jimmy Brown for a late winner in a 1957/58 League Cup Quarter-final tie.

Simpson again, this time out-jumping Bobby Evans to head Rangers' first goal past Dick Beattie in the Old Firm League encounter of 21 September 1957. Onlookers are Bertie Peacock and Sammy Baird. Celtic, however, eventually won 3-2.

Harry Melrose (arms raised) celebrates scoring his own second, and Rangers' fourth, in their 4-0 League Cup Semi-final win over Brechin City on 28 September 1957.

Billy Stevenson (1958-62). Wing half who won League and Cup medals on both sides of the border, in England with Liverpool.

Johnny Little (1951-62). Born Calgary, Alberta. A stylish full-back who won a full Scotland cap.

A crowd of 8,066 packed Station Park, Forfar for a Scottish Cup tie on 15 February 1958. Rangers romped to a 9-1 win, but on this occasion Max Murray's flying header bites the dust.

Rangers 1 Dundee 2 (20 September 1958). Sammy Baird's late consolation goal beats Bill Brown as Davie Wilson looks on. Rangers white strip with a red and blue band, together with blue satin shorts, was always a favourite with the fans, particularly in floodlight fixtures.

Max Murray scores Rangers' third goal in a 5-0 win over reigning champions Hearts on 14 December 1958.

Rangers Team Group 1958/59. From left to right, back row: McIlroy, Brand, Orr, Currie, Niven, Little, Martin, Moles, Austin, Wilson, McCorquodale. Middle row: S. Symon (Manager), Millar, Smith, Simpson, Valentine, Baird, Paterson, Telfer, Davies, Hogg, Neil, Murray, Craven (Assistant Trainer). Front row: Duncan, Scott, Queen, Shearer, McEwan, McColl, Stevenson, Caldow, Matthews, Hubbard, Provan.

Partick Thistle goalkeeper John Freebairn punches clear from Max Murray at Firhill as Rangers plunge to a shock 2-0 defeat in 1959.

Ian McMillan's late winner against Airdrieonians (2-1) on 21 January 1959 is acclaimed by Messrs Murray, Brand and Matthew.

Max Murray's eighty-eighth minute diving header, watched by Ralph Brand and Alex Scott, beats Motherwell's Hastie Weir to secure a 2-1 win.

Rangers and Arsenal have had a long and friendly association dating back to the nineteenth century days of Woolwich Arsenal. On 21 April 1959, Rangers scored a resounding 3-0 win at Highbury, and here George Niven watches a Mel Charles shot go over the crossbar.

Rangers 2 Dundee 0 (15 August 1959). Davie Wilson (on the left) turns away after scoring Rangers' second, acclaimed by George Duncan (7), Ian McMillan (8) and Jimmy Millar (9).

The closure of Third Lanark in 1967 has long been mourned by all football lovers, not just the faithful fans of the 'Hi-Hi'. Almost as old as Rangers, the club had a long and proud history, winning both the League Championship and Scottish Cup. Reproduced in the following pages are some scenes from 1950s meetings between the two clubs. This is the Glasgow Cup Final of September 1953 that saw Rangers win 3-0, and here John Prentice beats Jockie Robertson.

The famous old pavilion is prominent in this photograph of a Scottish Cup tie at Cathkin in 1954. Robertson sees this Rangers effort go wide in a goalless draw.

Robertson again defies a Rangers attack in the same Cup tie.

After a remarkable 4-4 draw at Ibrox, the two clubs returned to the same venue for a second replay. John Prentice heads the winning goal in a 3-2 win.

Once upon a time, there was an Ibrox railway station on the line from St Enoch's. Fans are shown here arriving for a game in the late-1950s.

RANGERS FOOTBALL CLUB

The world-famous Ibrox Trophy Room, opened in the late-1950s.

Nice v Rangers, 1956/57.

Rangers *v.* St Etienne, 1957/58.
Alex Scott during a raid on the
French goal.

Jimmy Millar and Sammy Baird on the attack against Eintracht Frankfurt in the 1959/60 European Cup Semi-final.

Harold Davis scores for Rangers against Ferencvaros in the very first European Cup Winners Cup tie of 1960/61.

114

Four
The Early Sixties

One of the great eras in Rangers' history, here are pictured the Rangers stars of the 1960/61 season.

Rangers swamped Ayr United 7-3 to clinch the 1960/61 Championship, and here Alex Scott scores with an overhead kick.

Eric Caldow (1952-66). A cultured full-back on either side of the park, Caldow was fast and skilful. Captain of both club and country for many years, a broken leg at Wembley in 1963 ended his international career.

Jimmy Millar (1955-67). The 'Old Warhorse'was a
centre forward of enormous courage and enthusiasm.
A tireless worker and originally a half-back, yet
scored 162 goals in 317 games for Rangers.

Billy Ritchie's dramatic last-minute penalty save from Pat Quinn secures Rangers' 2-1 win
over Motherwell on 28 February 1962.

Bobby Shearer (1955-65). 'Captain Cutlass'was a true 'bluenose' born and bred. An inspirational club captain and a hard-tackling full-back.

Billy Ritchie (1955-68). A consistent and reliable goalkeeper, perhaps his greatest save was that from Ron Flowers in the 1960/61 European Cup Winners Cup Semi-final at Molineaux.

An aerial view of Ibrox Stadium in the early 1960s.

The Albion Training Ground-now no longer with us. Seated here, from left to right: Davie Kinnear (Trainer), Joe Craven (Assistant Trainer), Scot Symon (Manager) and John F. Wilson Jnr (Director).

119

Davie Wilson (1956-67). Rangers' finest outside left since Alan Morton, Wilson was a goalscorer supreme, his total of 157 goals in 373 games a remarkable strike-rate for a winger.

Ronnie McKinnon (1959-73). Rangers' finest centre half since Willie Woodburn, Ronnie McKinnon was a skilful, intelligent player of poise and pace. At first weak in the air, he worked hard to improve his game in that field. Together with John Greig, he carried Rangers for much of the dark days of Celtic's glory years. A broken leg in Lisbon deprived him of the chance to savour European glory in Barcelona in 1972.

John Greig (Player 1960-78); (Manager 1978 –83). Perhaps the ultimate Rangers career, and arguably a club captain to compare with the great David Meiklejohn. A crowd of 65,000 attended his testimonial match – a British record unlikely to be bettered. Captain of club and country, he led Rangers to every domestic trophy and to European glory in Barcelona in 1972. Rangers' manager in later years, and now the club's public relations manager.

Willie Henderson (1960-72). 'Wee Willie' was a right-winger of startling skill, close ball control, and a great entertainer. He was also the scorer of some vital goals in Europe. One of the first players to wear contact lenses.

Jim Baxter (1960-65; 1969-70). A supreme talent, undoubtedly one of the greatest footballers
to ever wear the blue jersey, Baxter was the playmaker supreme of the great side of the early-
1960s. At his peak the finest player in Britain, and the best Rangers' left-sided player since
Alan Morton. 'Slim Jim' loved to play against Celtic and England. His displays at Wembley in
1963 and 1967 are legend.

Ralph Brand and Doug Baillie return from training. Brand was the supreme Rangers marksman, with 206 goals in 317 games. Baillie, a centre half signed from Airdrieonians, was a formidable figure for any opposing centre.

Ne'erday 1963, Rangers 4 Celtic 0. Goal no.1 – Harold Davis.

Goal no. 2 – Jimmy Millar.

124

Goal no. 3 – John Greig.

Goal no. 4 – Davie Wilson.

1964 Scottish Cup Final, Rangers 3 Dundee 1. A Dundee attack on the Rangers goal is thwarted. In picture is Bobby Shearer, John Greig, Billy Ritchie and David Provan (all on line), Ronnie McKinnon, Alan Gilzean, and behind goal, Andy Penman – in later years a Ranger. Rangers are wearing their change strip of blue and white stripes – or 'butcher stripes'

Wilson, Shearer, Millar and Henderson mob Ralph Brand after he had scored Rangers' third goal in the final minute. Brand's strike meant that he had created a new record by scoring in four consecutive Scottish Cup Finals (including the 1963 replay).

The Cup is won!

Acknowledgement

The author expresses his grateful thanks to Jack Murray for the use of certain photographs in this collection.